Please sign our guest book

&

share your experience with us and future guests

Wifi Password: ....

Host Contact Information: ....

Guest Name/s: ....

Check in Date: .... Check Out Date: ....

Traveled From: ....

Reason for the Trip: ....

Message To The Host:

Favorite Moments / Special Highlights

Places I/We Recommend - Restaurants - Entertainment - Must See Sights

⭐ ⭐ ⭐ ⭐ ⭐

Guest Name/s:
....

Check in Date: Check Out Date:
....

Traveled From:
....

Reason for the Trip:
....

Message To The Host:

[ ]

Favorite Moments / Special Highlights

[ ]

Places I/We Recommend - Restaurants - Entertainment - Must See Sights

[ ]

★ ★ ★ ★ ★

Guest Name/s:
....

Check in Date: .... Check Out Date: ....

Traveled From:
....

Reason for the Trip:
....

Message To The Host:

Favorite Moments / Special Highlights

Places I/We Recommend - Restaurants - Entertainment - Must See Sights

★ ★ ★ ★ ★

Guest Name/s:
....

Check in Date:
....

Check Out Date:
....

Traveled From
....

Reason for the Trip:
....

Message To The Host:

Favorite Moments / Special Highlights

Places I/We Recommend - Restaurants - Entertainment - Must See Sights

★ ★ ★ ★ ★

Guest Name/s:
....

Check in Date: Check Out Date:
....

Traveled From:
....

Reason for the Trip:
....

Message To The Host:

```
┌──────────────────────────────────────────────────────────┐
│                                                          │
│                                                          │
│                                                          │
│                                                          │
│                                                          │
└──────────────────────────────────────────────────────────┘
```

Favorite Moments / Special Highlights

```
┌──────────────────────────────────────────────────────────┐
│                                                          │
│                                                          │
│                                                          │
│                                                          │
└──────────────────────────────────────────────────────────┘
```

Places I/We Recommend - Restaurants - Entertainment - Must See Sights

```
┌──────────────────────────────────────────────────────────┐
│                                                          │
│                                                          │
│                                                          │
│                                                          │
└──────────────────────────────────────────────────────────┘
```

★ ★ ★ ★ ★

Guest Name/s:
....

Check in Date: .... Check Out Date: ....

Traveled From:
....

Reason for the Trip: ....

Message To The Host:

Favorite Moments / Special Highlights

Places I/We Recommend - Restaurants - Entertainment - Must See Sights

★ ★ ★ ★ ★

Guest Name/s: ....

Check in Date: .... Check Out Date: ....

Traveled From: ....

Reason for the Trip: ....

Message To The Host:

[ ]

Favorite Moments / Special Highlights

[ ]

Places I/We Recommend - Restaurants - Entertainment - Must See Sights

[ ]

★ ★ ★ ★ ★

Guest Name/s: ....

Check in Date: .... Check Out Date: ....

Traveled From: ....

Reason for the Trip: ....

Message To The Host:

```



```

Favorite Moments / Special Highlights

```



```

Places I/We Recommend - Restaurants - Entertainment - Must See Sights

```



```

★ ★ ★ ★ ★

Guest Name/s:
....

Check in Date: .... Check Out Date: ....

Traveled From:

Reason for the Trip: ....

Message To The Host:

Favorite Moments / Special Highlights

Places I/We Recommend - Restaurants - Entertainment - Must See Sights

⭐ ⭐ ⭐ ⭐ ⭐

Guest Name/s:

Check in Date: .... Check Out Date: ....

Traveled From: ....

Reason for the Trip: ....

Message To The Host:

Favorite Moments / Special Highlights

Places I/We Recommend - Restaurants - Entertainment - Must See Sights

★ ★ ★ ★ ★

Guest Name/s:
....

Check in Date: Check Out Date:
....

Traveled From:
....

Reason for the Trip:
....

Message To The Host:

[ ]

Favorite Moments / Special Highlights

[ ]

Places I/We Recommend - Restaurants - Entertainment - Must See Sights

[ ]

★ ★ ★ ★ ★

Guest Name/s:
....

Check in Date: Check Out Date:
....

Traveled From:
....

Reason for the Trip:
....

Message To The Host:

```
                                                                    
                                                                    
                                                                    
                                                                    
                                                                    
```

Favorite Moments / Special Highlights

```
                                                                    
                                                                    
                                                                    
                                                                    
```

Places I/We Recommend - Restaurants - Entertainment - Must See Sights

```
                                                                    
                                                                    
                                                                    
```

★ ★ ★ ★ ★

Guest Name/s: ....

Check in Date: .... Check Out Date: ....

Traveled From: ....

Reason for the Trip: ....

Message To The Host:

Favorite Moments / Special Highlights

Places I/We Recommend - Restaurants - Entertainment - Must See Sights

★ ★ ★ ★ ★

Guest Name/s:
....

Check in Date:
....

Check Out Date:
....

Traveled From:
....

Reason for the Trip:
....

Message To The Host:

Favorite Moments / Special Highlights

Places I/We Recommend - Restaurants - Entertainment - Must See Sights

★ ★ ★ ★ ★

Guest Name/s: ....

Check in Date: .... Check Out Date: ....

Traveled From: ....

Reason for the Trip: ....

Message To The Host:

Favorite Moments / Special Highlights

Places I/We Recommend - Restaurants - Entertainment - Must See Sights

★ ★ ★ ★ ★

Guest Name/s: ....

Check in Date: .... Check Out Date: ....

Traveled From: ....

Reason for the Trip: ....

Message To The Host:

```
[                                                              ]
```

Favorite Moments / Special Highlights

```
[                                                              ]
```

Places I/We Recommend - Restaurants - Entertainment - Must See Sights

```
[                                                              ]
```

★ ★ ★ ★ ★

Guest Name/s: ....

Check in Date: .... Check Out Date: ....

Traveled From: ....

Reason for the Trip: ....

Message To The Host:

[ ]

Favorite Moments / Special Highlights

[ ]

Places I/We Recommend - Restaurants - Entertainment - Must See Sights

[ ]

★ ★ ★ ★ ★

Guest Name/s:
....

Check in Date: .... Check Out Date: ....

Traveled From: ....

Reason for the Trip: ....

Message To The Host:

```


```

Favorite Moments / Special Highlights

```


```

Places I/We Recommend - Restaurants - Entertainment - Must See Sights

```


```

★ ★ ★ ★ ★

Guest Name/s:
....

Check in Date: Check Out Date:
....

Traveled From:
....

Reason for the Trip:
....

Message To The Host:

Favorite Moments / Special Highlights

Places I/We Recommend - Restaurants - Entertainment - Must See Sights

★ ★ ★ ★ ★

Guest Name/s:
....

Check in Date:
....

Check Out Date:
....

Traveled From:

Reason for the Trip:
....

Message To The Host:

Favorite Moments / Special Highlights

Places I/We Recommend - Restaurants - Entertainment - Must See Sights

★ ★ ★ ★ ★

Guest Name/s:

Check in Date: .... Check Out Date: ....

Traveled From: ....

Reason for the Trip: ....

Message To The Host:

Favorite Moments / Special Highlights

Places I/We Recommend - Restaurants - Entertainment - Must See Sights

★ ★ ★ ★ ★

Guest Name/s: ....

Check in Date: .... Check Out Date: ....

Traveled From: ....

Reason for the Trip: ....

Message To The Host:

Favorite Moments / Special Highlights

Places I/We Recommend - Restaurants - Entertainment - Must See Sights

★ ★ ★ ★ ★

Guest Name/s:
....

Check in Date:
....

Check Out Date:
....

Traveled From:
....

Reason for the Trip:
....

Message To The Host:

Favorite Moments / Special Highlights

Places I/We Recommend - Restaurants - Entertainment - Must See Sights

★ ★ ★ ★ ★

Guest Name/s:
....

Check in Date: .... Check Out Date: ....

Traveled From:
....

Reason for the Trip:
....

Message To The Host:

_____

Favorite Moments / Special Highlights

_____

Places I/We Recommend - Restaurants - Entertainment - Must See Sights

_____

⭐ ⭐ ⭐ ⭐ ⭐

Guest Name/s:
....

Check in Date: .... Check Out Date: ....

Traveled From: ....

Reason for the Trip: ....

Message To The Host:

[ ]

Favorite Moments / Special Highlights

[ ]

Places I/We Recommend - Restaurants - Entertainment - Must See Sights

[ ]

★ ★ ★ ★ ★

Guest Name/s: ....

Check in Date: .... Check Out Date: ....

Traveled From: ....

Reason for the Trip: ....

Message To The Host:

[ ]

Favorite Moments / Special Highlights

[ ]

Places I/We Recommend - Restaurants - Entertainment - Must See Sights

[ ]

★ ★ ★ ★ ★

Guest Name/s: ....

Check in Date: .... Check Out Date: ....

Traveled From: ....

Reason for the Trip: ....

Message To The Host:

```

```

Favorite Moments / Special Highlights

```

```

Places I/We Recommend - Restaurants - Entertainment - Must See Sights

```

```

★ ★ ★ ★ ★

Guest Name/s:
....

Check in Date:
....

Check Out Date:
....

Traveled From:
....

Reason for the Trip:
....

Message To The Host:

Favorite Moments / Special Highlights

Places I/We Recommend - Restaurants - Entertainment - Must See Sights

★ ★ ★ ★ ★

Guest Name/s:
....

Check in Date: .... Check Out Date: ....

Traveled From: ....

Reason for the Trip: ....

Message To The Host:

```



```

Favorite Moments / Special Highlights

```



```

Places I/We Recommend - Restaurants - Entertainment - Must See Sights

```



```

★ ★ ★ ★ ★

Guest Name/s: ....

Check in Date: .... Check Out Date: ....

Traveled From: ....

Reason for the Trip: ....

Message To The Host:

Favorite Moments / Special Highlights

Places I/We Recommend - Restaurants - Entertainment - Must See Sights

★ ★ ★ ★ ★

Guest Name/s: ....

Check in Date: .... Check Out Date: ....

Traveled From:

Reason for the Trip: ....

Message To The Host:

Favorite Moments / Special Highlights

Places I/We Recommend - Restaurants - Entertainment - Must See Sights

★ ★ ★ ★ ★

Guest Name/s:

Check in Date: .... Check Out Date: ....

Traveled From: ....

Reason for the Trip: ....

Message To The Host:

Favorite Moments / Special Highlights

Places I/We Recommend - Restaurants - Entertainment - Must See Sights

★ ★ ★ ★ ★

Guest Name/s: ....

Check in Date: .... Check Out Date: ....

Traveled From: ....

Reason for the Trip: ....

Message To The Host:

Favorite Moments / Special Highlights

Places I/We Recommend - Restaurants - Entertainment - Must See Sights

★ ★ ★ ★ ★

Guest Name/s: ....

Check in Date: .... Check Out Date: ....

Traveled From: ....

Reason for the Trip: ....

Message To The Host:

Favorite Moments / Special Highlights

Places I/We Recommend - Restaurants - Entertainment - Must See Sights

⭐ ⭐ ⭐ ⭐ ⭐

Guest Name/s: ....

Check in Date: .... Check Out Date: ....

Traveled From: ....

Reason for the Trip: ....

Message To The Host:

```
┌─────────────────────────────────────────────────────────┐
│                                                         │
│                                                         │
│                                                         │
│                                                         │
└─────────────────────────────────────────────────────────┘
```

Favorite Moments / Special Highlights

```
┌─────────────────────────────────────────────────────────┐
│                                                         │
│                                                         │
│                                                         │
│                                                         │
└─────────────────────────────────────────────────────────┘
```

Places I/We Recommend - Restaurants - Entertainment - Must See Sights

```
┌─────────────────────────────────────────────────────────┐
│                                                         │
│                                                         │
│                                                         │
│                                                         │
└─────────────────────────────────────────────────────────┘
```

★ ★ ★ ★ ★

Guest Name/s:
....

Check in Date: .... Check Out Date: ....

Traveled From:
....

Reason for the Trip:
....

Message To The Host:

Favorite Moments / Special Highlights

Places I/We Recommend - Restaurants - Entertainment - Must See Sights

★ ★ ★ ★ ★

Guest Name/s: ....

Check in Date: ....   Check Out Date: ....

Traveled From: ....

Reason for the Trip: ....

Message To The Host:

Favorite Moments / Special Highlights

Places I/We Recommend - Restaurants - Entertainment - Must See Sights

⭐ ⭐ ⭐ ⭐ ⭐

Guest Name/s:
....

Check in Date:
....

Check Out Date:
....

Traveled From:
....

Reason for the Trip:
....

Message To The Host:

Favorite Moments / Special Highlights

Places I/We Recommend - Restaurants - Entertainment - Must See Sights

★ ★ ★ ★ ★

Guest Name/s: ....

Check in Date: .... Check Out Date: ....

Traveled From: ....

Reason for the Trip: ....

Message To The Host:

```

```

Favorite Moments / Special Highlights

```

```

Places I/We Recommend - Restaurants - Entertainment - Must See Sights

```

```

★ ★ ★ ★ ★

Guest Name/s: ....

Check in Date: .... Check Out Date: ....

Traveled From: ....

Reason for the Trip: ....

Message To The Host:

Favorite Moments / Special Highlights

Places I/We Recommend - Restaurants - Entertainment - Must See Sights

★ ★ ★ ★ ★

Guest Name/s: ....

Check in Date: .... Check Out Date: ....

Traveled From: ....

Reason for the Trip: ....

Message To The Host:

Favorite Moments / Special Highlights

Places I/We Recommend - Restaurants - Entertainment - Must See Sights

★ ★ ★ ★ ★

Guest Name/s:
....

Check in Date: .... Check Out Date: ....

Traveled From:

Reason for the Trip:
....

Message To The Host:

....

Favorite Moments / Special Highlights

Places I/We Recommend - Restaurants - Entertainment - Must See Sights

★ ★ ★ ★ ★

Guest Name/s:

Check in Date: .... Check Out Date: ....

Traveled From: ....

Reason for the Trip: ....

Message To The Host:

Favorite Moments / Special Highlights

Places I/We Recommend - Restaurants - Entertainment - Must See Sights

⭐ ⭐ ⭐ ⭐ ⭐

Guest Name/s:

....

Check in Date:

....

Check Out Date:

....

Traveled From:

....

Reason for the Trip:

....

Message To The Host:

Favorite Moments / Special Highlights

Places I/We Recommend - Restaurants - Entertainment - Must See Sights

★ ★ ★ ★ ★

Guest Name/s: ....

Check in Date: ....   Check Out Date: ....

Traveled From: ....

Reason for the Trip: ....

Message To The Host:

Favorite Moments / Special Highlights

Places I/We Recommend - Restaurants - Entertainment - Must See Sights

⭐ ⭐ ⭐ ⭐ ⭐

Guest Name/s:
....

Check in Date:
....

Check Out Date:
....

Traveled From:
....

Reason for the Trip:
....

Message To The Host:

Favorite Moments / Special Highlights

Places I/We Recommend - Restaurants - Entertainment - Must See Sights

★ ★ ★ ★ ★

Guest Name/s: ....

Check in Date: .... Check Out Date: ....

Traveled From: ....

Reason for the Trip: ....

Message To The Host:

Favorite Moments / Special Highlights

Places I/We Recommend - Restaurants - Entertainment - Must See Sights

★ ★ ★ ★ ★

Guest Name/s:
....

Check in Date:
....

Check Out Date:
....

Traveled From:
....

Reason for the Trip:
....

Message To The Host:

Favorite Moments / Special Highlights

Places I/We Recommend - Restaurants - Entertainment - Must See Sights

★ ★ ★ ★ ★

Guest Name/s: ....

Check in Date: ....   Check Out Date: ....

Traveled From: ....

Reason for the Trip: ....

Message To The Host:

Favorite Moments / Special Highlights

Places I/We Recommend - Restaurants - Entertainment - Must See Sights

---

★ ★ ★ ★ ★

Guest Name/s:
....

Check in Date: .... Check Out Date: ....

Traveled From:
....

Reason for the Trip:
....

Message To The Host:

Favorite Moments / Special Highlights

Places I/We Recommend - Restaurants - Entertainment - Must See Sights

★ ★ ★ ★ ★

Guest Name/s: ....

Check in Date: ....   Check Out Date: ....

Traveled From: ....

Reason for the Trip: ....

Message To The Host:

| |
| |

Favorite Moments / Special Highlights

| |
| |

Places I/We Recommend - Restaurants - Entertainment - Must See Sights

| |
| |

Guest Name/s:
....

Check in Date:
....

Check Out Date:
....

Traveled From:
....

Reason for the Trip:
....

Message To The Host:

Favorite Moments / Special Highlights

Places I/We Recommend - Restaurants - Entertainment - Must See Sights

★ ★ ★ ★ ★

Guest Name/s: ....

Check in Date: .... Check Out Date: ....

Traveled From:

Reason for the Trip: ....

Message To The Host:

....

Favorite Moments / Special Highlights

Places I/We Recommend - Restaurants - Entertainment - Must See Sights

★ ★ ★ ★ ★

Guest Name/s:

Check in Date: .... Check Out Date: ....

Traveled From: ....

Reason for the Trip: ....

Message To The Host:

Favorite Moments / Special Highlights

Places I/We Recommend - Restaurants - Entertainment - Must See Sights

★ ★ ★ ★ ★

Guest Name/s: ....

Check in Date: .... Check Out Date: ....

Traveled From: ....

Reason for the Trip: ....

Message To The Host:

```



```

Favorite Moments / Special Highlights

```



```

Places I/We Recommend - Restaurants - Entertainment - Must See Sights

```



```

★ ★ ★ ★ ★

Guest Name/s:
....

Check in Date:
....

Check Out Date:
....

Traveled From:
....

Reason for the Trip:
....

Message To The Host:

Favorite Moments / Special Highlights

Places I/We Recommend - Restaurants - Entertainment - Must See Sights

★ ★ ★ ★ ★

Guest Name/s: ....

Check in Date: .... Check Out Date: ....

Traveled From: ....

Reason for the Trip: ....

Message To The Host:

Favorite Moments / Special Highlights

Places I/We Recommend - Restaurants - Entertainment - Must See Sights

Guest Name/s:
....

Check in Date: .... Check Out Date: ....

Traveled From: ....

Reason for the Trip: ....

Message To The Host:

Favorite Moments / Special Highlights

Places I/We Recommend - Restaurants - Entertainment - Must See Sights

★ ★ ★ ★ ★

Guest Name/s: ....

Check in Date: .... Check Out Date: ....

Traveled From: ....

Reason for the Trip: ....

Message To The Host:

Favorite Moments / Special Highlights

Places I/We Recommend - Restaurants - Entertainment - Must See Sights

Guest Name/s: ....

Check in Date: .... Check Out Date: ....

Traveled From: ....

Reason for the Trip: ....

Message To The Host:

Favorite Moments / Special Highlights

Places I/We Recommend - Restaurants - Entertainment - Must See Sights

★ ★ ★ ★ ★

Guest Name/s:
....

Check in Date: .... Check Out Date: ....

Traveled From:
....

Reason for the Trip:
....

Message To The Host:

Favorite Moments / Special Highlights

Places I/We Recommend - Restaurants - Entertainment - Must See Sights

Guest Name/s:
....

Check in Date: Check Out Date:
....

Traveled From:
....

Reason for the Trip:
....

Message To The Host:

Favorite Moments / Special Highlights

Places I/We Recommend - Restaurants - Entertainment - Must See Sights

★ ★ ★ ★ ★

Guest Name/s: ....

Check in Date: ....   Check Out Date: ....

Traveled From: ....

Reason for the Trip: ....

Message To The Host:

Favorite Moments / Special Highlights

Places I/We Recommend - Restaurants - Entertainment - Must See Sights

★ ★ ★ ★ ★

Guest Name/s:
....

Check in Date: .... Check Out Date: ....

Traveled From:

Reason for the Trip: ....

Message To The Host:

....

Favorite Moments / Special Highlights

Places I/We Recommend - Restaurants - Entertainment - Must See Sights

★ ★ ★ ★ ★

Guest Name/s:

Check in Date: .... Check Out Date: ....

Traveled From: ....

Reason for the Trip: ....

Message To The Host:

Favorite Moments / Special Highlights

Places I/We Recommend - Restaurants - Entertainment - Must See Sights

Guest Name/s: ....

Check in Date: ....   Check Out Date: ....

Traveled From: ....

Reason for the Trip: ....

Message To The Host:

```

```

Favorite Moments / Special Highlights

```

```

Places I/We Recommend - Restaurants - Entertainment - Must See Sights

```

```

★ ★ ★ ★ ★

Guest Name/s: ....

Check in Date: .... Check Out Date: ....

Traveled From: ....

Reason for the Trip: ....

Message To The Host:

Favorite Moments / Special Highlights

Places I/We Recommend - Restaurants - Entertainment - Must See Sights

★ ★ ★ ★ ★

Guest Name/s: ....

Check in Date: .... Check Out Date: ....

Traveled From: ....

Reason for the Trip: ....

Message To The Host:

Favorite Moments / Special Highlights

Places I/We Recommend - Restaurants - Entertainment - Must See Sights

★ ★ ★ ★ ★

Guest Name/s: ....

Check in Date: .... Check Out Date: ....

Traveled From: ....

Reason for the Trip: ....

Message To The Host:

Favorite Moments / Special Highlights

Places I/We Recommend - Restaurants - Entertainment - Must See Sights

★ ★ ★ ★ ★

Guest Name/s:
....

Check in Date:
....

Check Out Date:
....

Traveled From:
....

Reason for the Trip:
....

Message To The Host:

Favorite Moments / Special Highlights

Places I/We Recommend - Restaurants - Entertainment - Must See Sights

★ ★ ★ ★ ★

Guest Name/s:
....

Check in Date:
....

Check Out Date:
....

Traveled From:
....

Reason for the Trip:
....

Message To The Host:

Favorite Moments / Special Highlights

Places I/We Recommend - Restaurants - Entertainment - Must See Sights

★ ★ ★ ★ ★

Guest Name/s: ....

Check in Date: .... Check Out Date: ....

Traveled From: ....

Reason for the Trip: ....

Message To The Host:

Favorite Moments / Special Highlights

Places I/We Recommend - Restaurants - Entertainment - Must See Sights

★ ★ ★ ★ ★

Guest Name/s: ....

Check in Date: .... Check Out Date: ....

Traveled From: ....

Reason for the Trip: ....

Message To The Host:

Favorite Moments / Special Highlights

Places I/We Recommend - Restaurants - Entertainment - Must See Sights

★ ★ ★ ★ ★

Guest Name/s:
....

Check in Date: .... Check Out Date: ....

Traveled From:
....

Reason for the Trip:
....

Message To The Host:

Favorite Moments / Special Highlights

Places I/We Recommend - Restaurants - Entertainment - Must See Sights

★ ★ ★ ★ ★

Guest Name/s: ....

Check in Date: .... Check Out Date: ....

Traveled From:

Reason for the Trip: ....

Message To The Host:

....

Favorite Moments / Special Highlights

Places I/We Recommend - Restaurants - Entertainment - Must See Sights

★ ★ ★ ★ ★

Guest Name/s:

Check in Date: .... Check Out Date: ....

Traveled From: ....

Reason for the Trip: ....

Message To The Host:

Favorite Moments / Special Highlights

Places I/We Recommend - Restaurants - Entertainment - Must See Sights

★ ★ ★ ★ ★

Guest Name/s: ....

Check in Date: .... Check Out Date: ....

Traveled From: ....

Reason for the Trip: ....

Message To The Host:

Favorite Moments / Special Highlights

Places I/We Recommend - Restaurants - Entertainment - Must See Sights

★ ★ ★ ★ ★

Guest Name/s:
....

Check in Date:
....

Check Out Date:
....

Traveled From:
....

Reason for the Trip:
....

Message To The Host:

[ ]

Favorite Moments / Special Highlights

[ ]

Places I/We Recommend - Restaurants - Entertainment - Must See Sights

[ ]

★ ★ ★ ★ ★

Guest Name/s: ....

Check in Date: ....   Check Out Date: ....

Traveled From: ....

Reason for the Trip: ....

Message To The Host:

Favorite Moments / Special Highlights

Places I/We Recommend - Restaurants - Entertainment - Must See Sights

⭐ ⭐ ⭐ ⭐ ⭐

Guest Name/s: ....

Check in Date: .... Check Out Date: ....

Traveled From: ....

Reason for the Trip: ....

Message To The Host:

Favorite Moments / Special Highlights

Places I/We Recommend - Restaurants - Entertainment - Must See Sights

★ ★ ★ ★ ★

Guest Name/s: ....

Check in Date: .... Check Out Date: ....

Traveled From: ....

Reason for the Trip: ....

Message To The Host:

Favorite Moments / Special Highlights

Places I/We Recommend - Restaurants - Entertainment - Must See Sights

★ ★ ★ ★ ★

Guest Name/s: ....

Check in Date: .... Check Out Date: ....

Traveled From: ....

Reason for the Trip: ....

Message To The Host:

[ ]

Favorite Moments / Special Highlights

[ ]

Places I/We Recommend - Restaurants - Entertainment - Must See Sights

[ ]

★ ★ ★ ★ ★

Guest Name/s: ....

Check in Date: .... Check Out Date: ....

Traveled From: ....

Reason for the Trip: ....

Message To The Host:

```




```

Favorite Moments / Special Highlights

```




```

Places I/We Recommend - Restaurants - Entertainment - Must See Sights

```




```

★ ★ ★ ★ ★

Guest Name/s:
....

Check in Date:
....

Check Out Date:
....

Traveled From:
....

Reason for the Trip:
....

Message To The Host:

Favorite Moments / Special Highlights

Places I/We Recommend - Restaurants - Entertainment - Must See Sights

★ ★ ★ ★ ★

Guest Name/s: ....

Check in Date: .... Check Out Date: ....

Traveled From: ....

Reason for the Trip: ....

Message To The Host:

[ ]

Favorite Moments / Special Highlights

[ ]

Places I/We Recommend - Restaurants - Entertainment - Must See Sights

[ ]

⭐ ⭐ ⭐ ⭐ ⭐

Guest Name/s: ....

Check in Date: ....   Check Out Date: ....

Traveled From:

Reason for the Trip: ....

Message To The Host:

Favorite Moments / Special Highlights

Places I/We Recommend - Restaurants - Entertainment - Must See Sights

★ ★ ★ ★ ★

Guest Name/s:

Check in Date: .... Check Out Date: ....

Traveled From: ....

Reason for the Trip: ....

Message To The Host:

Favorite Moments / Special Highlights

Places I/We Recommend - Restaurants - Entertainment - Must See Sights

Guest Name/s:
....

Check in Date:
....

Check Out Date:
....

Traveled From:
....

Reason for the Trip:
....

Message To The Host:

Favorite Moments / Special Highlights

Places I/We Recommend - Restaurants - Entertainment - Must See Sights

★ ★ ★ ★ ★

Guest Name/s: ....

Check in Date: .... Check Out Date: ....

Traveled From: ....

Reason for the Trip: ....

Message To The Host:

Favorite Moments / Special Highlights

Places I/We Recommend - Restaurants - Entertainment - Must See Sights

⭐ ⭐ ⭐ ⭐ ⭐

Guest Name/s: ....

Check in Date: .... Check Out Date: ....

Traveled From: ....

Reason for the Trip: ....

Message To The Host:

```



```

Favorite Moments / Special Highlights

```



```

Places I/We Recommend - Restaurants - Entertainment - Must See Sights

```



```

⭐ ⭐ ⭐ ⭐ ⭐

Guest Name/s: ....

Check in Date: .... Check Out Date: ....

Traveled From: ....

Reason for the Trip: ....

Message To The Host:

Favorite Moments / Special Highlights

Places I/We Recommend - Restaurants - Entertainment - Must See Sights

★ ★ ★ ★ ★

Guest Name/s:
....

Check in Date: .... Check Out Date: ....

Traveled From: ....

Reason for the Trip: ....

Message To The Host:

Favorite Moments / Special Highlights

Places I/We Recommend - Restaurants - Entertainment - Must See Sights

★ ★ ★ ★ ★

Guest Name/s: ....

Check in Date: .... Check Out Date: ....

Traveled From: ....

Reason for the Trip: ....

Message To The Host:

Favorite Moments / Special Highlights

Places I/We Recommend - Restaurants - Entertainment - Must See Sights

Guest Name/s:
....

Check in Date:
....

Check Out Date:
....

Traveled From:
....

Reason for the Trip:
....

Message To The Host:

Favorite Moments / Special Highlights

Places I/We Recommend - Restaurants - Entertainment - Must See Sights

★ ★ ★ ★ ★

Guest Name/s: ....

Check in Date: .... Check Out Date: ....

Traveled From: ....

Reason for the Trip: ....

Message To The Host:

(blank box)

Favorite Moments / Special Highlights

(blank box)

Places I/We Recommend - Restaurants - Entertainment - Must See Sights

(blank box)

⭐ ⭐ ⭐ ⭐ ⭐

Guest Name/s: ....

Check in Date: .... Check Out Date: ....

Traveled From: ....

Reason for the Trip: ....

Message To The Host:

Favorite Moments / Special Highlights

Places I/We Recommend - Restaurants - Entertainment - Must See Sights

★ ★ ★ ★ ★

Guest Name/s: ....

Check in Date: .... Check Out Date: ....

Traveled From:

Reason for the Trip: ....

Message To The Host:

Favorite Moments / Special Highlights

Places I/We Recommend - Restaurants - Entertainment - Must See Sights

⭐ ⭐ ⭐ ⭐ ⭐

Guest Name/s:

Check in Date: .... Check Out Date: ....

Traveled From: ....

Reason for the Trip: ....

Message To The Host:

Favorite Moments / Special Highlights

Places I/We Recommend - Restaurants - Entertainment - Must See Sights

★ ★ ★ ★ ★

Guest Name/s: ....

Check in Date: .... Check Out Date: ....

Traveled From: ....

Reason for the Trip: ....

Message To The Host:

```



```

Favorite Moments / Special Highlights

```



```

Places I/We Recommend - Restaurants - Entertainment - Must See Sights

```



```

⭐ ⭐ ⭐ ⭐ ⭐

Guest Name/s:
....

Check in Date:
....

Check Out Date:
....

Traveled From:
....

Reason for the Trip:
....

Message To The Host:

Favorite Moments / Special Highlights

Places I/We Recommend - Restaurants - Entertainment - Must See Sights

★ ★ ★ ★ ★

Made in the USA
Monee, IL
10 July 2022

99436567R00057